The
War of 1812

Jill K. Mulhall, M.Ed.

Table of Contents

Fighting for Respect

The Treaty of Paris ended the Revolutionary War in 1783. The United States had won its freedom from Great Britain. But America still did not have the respect of the world. Other countries took advantage of the new nation. In less than 30 years, America was at war with Great Britain again. The people called this their second war for **independence**.

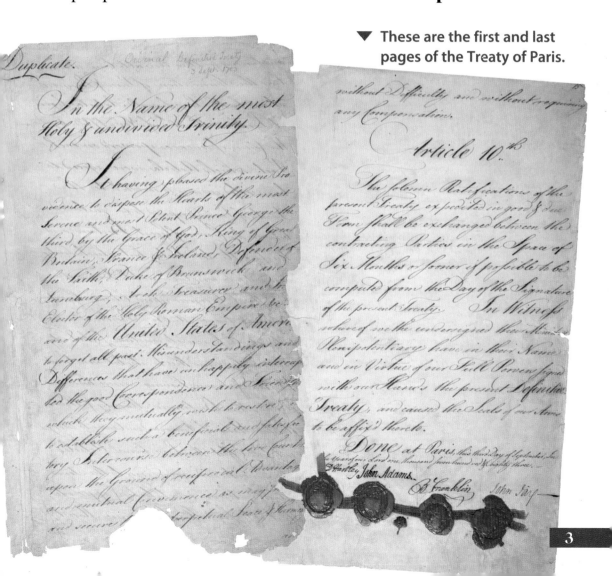

▼ **These are the first and last pages of the Treaty of Paris.**

The Embargo Act

President Thomas Jefferson wanted to stop the problems at sea. In 1807, he asked Congress to pass an **embargo** (im-BAR-go). This made it against the law for American ships to carry goods to any other country. The plan was to make the people in Great Britain and France miss American products. But, the Europeans found goods elsewhere. It was only American businesses that suffered.

▲ The new capital city had a large home for the president.

Problems of a New Nation

The early 1800s were a proud time for Americans. They had beaten powerful Great Britain to win their independence. Their government was a unique **democracy** (duh-MOK-ruh-see). They were building a new capital city in Washington, D.C.

At first, the world did not expect much from the new country. The Americans worked hard to change that. They sent **ambassadors** (am-BAS-uh-duhrs) to other countries. These men told the world about the crops and goods that the Americans had to trade.

Soon, Americans were trading with countries in Europe, Asia, Africa, and South America. To do this, they built many new ships. By 1800, America had even more ships at sea than Great Britain, the "Ruler of the Seas."

Great Britain and France did not like this. They wanted to control shipping. British and French ships began to stop American ships on the open seas. Sometimes they would take goods. Other times they would **seize** (SEEZ) a whole ship or sink it. This made Americans very angry.

Crimes at Sea

Great Britain took more than goods from American ships. They also took American men. The British navy was short of men. Many sailors had **deserted** (di-ZERT-ed) their navy. The British began stopping ships to look for these men. But many times the men they captured were really from the United States. These men were then **impressed**, or forced to join the British navy.

▼ Sailors being forced to join the British navy.

Trouble in the West

Great Britain caused other troubles for America. The Revolutionary War had driven the British from the colonies. But they still held land just north of the United States, in Canada. They also had several military forts there.

The Ohio River Valley was a large **territory** (TAIR-uh-tor-ee) between the United States and Canada. After the Revolutionary War, American settlers began to move into this area. The problem was that many American Indians already lived there. They had treaties promising them the land. The British had told them they would always be able to live there.

Shawnee Leader

The Indians found a great leader in a man named Tecumseh (tuh-KUM-suh). He was a Shawnee Indian from western Ohio. Tecumseh was a fierce warrior. He led many war parties against the white settlers. Tecumseh also gave powerful speeches about Indian rights. He organized the Indians. He said if they worked together they could get rid of the settlers.

Sneak Attack

Tecumseh formed a settlement near the Tippecanoe (tip-uh-kuh-NEW) River. Many unhappy Indians joined him there. They warned the government that they would fight against the loss of their land. In 1811, Tecumseh took a short trip away from the village. While he was away, William Henry Harrison led an army to the village. They destroyed it and made the Indians leave.

▲ **William Henry Harrison in battle**

The United States government did not listen to the Indians' complaints. Frustrated, the Indians turned to their old friends in Canada. The British were happy to help. They gave the Indians guns and ammunition. The British encouraged the Indians to attack the American settlers.

The British hoped they could eventually get some of this territory for Canada. They also wanted to protect their fur trade. The frontier became a very dangerous place. The American settlers begged their government to protect them.

Calling for War

As years went by, Americans became more and more angry. They were proud of their young country. But they felt that Great Britain was showing them no respect.

Businessmen were upset about the money they lost when ships were stopped at sea. Sailors' families worried about

A New Reason to Fight

In 1807, the British frigate (FRI-guht) *Leopard* went searching for deserters. They found the American ship *Chesapeake* off the coast of Virginia. The British captain demanded to search the American ship. The American captain refused. The *Leopard* opened fire. Three American sailors were killed. Others were impressed by the British. This was the last straw for many Americans.

▼ These American sailors are being impressed after the battle between the *Leopard* and *Chesapeake*.

their sons or husbands being impressed. They began to call for a war against Britain. Their **slogan** was "Free Trade and Sailors' Rights."

Out West, the settlers feared attacks by the Indians or the British army. They wanted to strike to the north. "On to Canada!" they cried.

Not everyone wanted to fight, however. Many people in New England and New York had jobs in shipping. They disliked the idea of a war. They knew it would shut down businesses.

James Madison became the fourth president of the United States in 1809. He hoped to avoid war. He thought the American navy had too few ships. The army was small and untrained. He did not think America could win a war against Great Britain.

President James Madison

An Old Friend

Great Britain was not the only country that seized American ships. France did so as well. Both countries were guilty of hurting American trade. But the British took most of the blame. People remembered how France had helped the United States in the Revolutionary War. They wanted to give the French the benefit of the doubt.

War Hawks in Washington

Americans were split about whether to declare war. They needed a push in one direction or the other. That push came from a group of men called the War Hawks.

The War Hawks were **politicians** (pol-uh-TISH-uhns) from the West and the South. Many of them were elected to Congress at the same time. They came to Washington in 1811. The men were young and outspoken. They argued passionately for war.

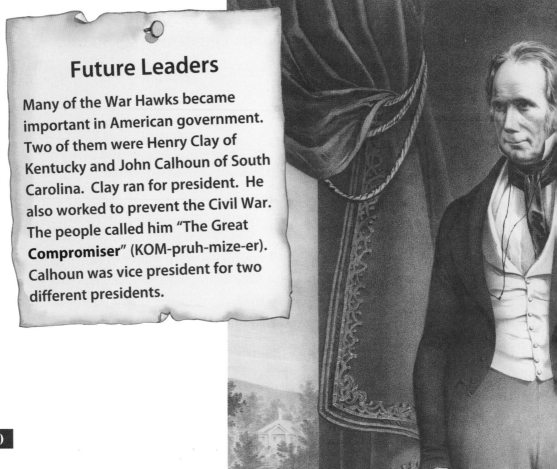

Future Leaders

Many of the War Hawks became important in American government. Two of them were Henry Clay of Kentucky and John Calhoun of South Carolina. Clay ran for president. He also worked to prevent the Civil War. The people called him "The Great Compromiser" (KOM-pruh-mize-er). Calhoun was vice president for two different presidents.

These men were eager to take on Great Britain. They said it was a matter of national pride. They thought that Great Britain treated Americans badly. If Americans did not fight back, they might lose the respect of the world.

The War Hawks argued in Congress for the war. At the same time, Congress strengthened the navy and the army.

On June 18, 1812, Congress declared war on Great Britain. By now, President Madison agreed with the decision to go to war. He said, "Peace as we now have it is disgraceful, and war **honorable**."

John Calhoun

Secret Plans

The War Hawks used **nationalism** (NASH-uh-nuhl-iz-uhm) as a reason to fight. But they also had other reasons. They wanted new lands for the United States. The men from the West hoped to take over Canada. The men from the South wanted to capture Florida and Texas. They used the problems with Great Britain as an excuse to go after these lands.

◀ Henry Clay, "The Great Compromiser"

On to Canada!

The War Hawks said America would win the war in 30 days. That was silly. The United States Army was small and untrained. The navy had good ships. But there were only 20 of them. America did have one thing going for it. Great Britain was already at war with France. Its best soldiers were busy.

The American military leaders decided to attack Canada. They wanted to get rid of the British army there. Then, they thought the people of Canada would come and help the United States.

A Bright Spot

The army did badly in 1812. But the navy was a different story. It had several victories at sea. The American ship *Constitution* defeated two British ships, *Guerriere* and *Java*. During one battle, an American sailor on the *Constitution* watched a cannonball bounce right off the side of his ship. He nicknamed the ship "Old Ironsides." The name stuck.

▼ The *Constitution* in battle

The British navy had one sure way to keep their advantage at sea. They set up a giant blockade of the East Coast. No ships could get in or out of the American ports. Farmers and merchants could not get their goods to market. The United States Navy could not seek out any battles. Britain reminded Americans of who really controlled the seas.

▲ William Hull took too long to make important military decisions.

Two attacks into Canada from New York ended quickly. Another try started from Detroit, Michigan. It failed because of the general in charge, William Hull. He was too careful and slow. He failed to capture a British fort and had to **surrender** (suh-REN-duhr) the American fort, Fort Detroit!

The public was unhappy with the way the war was going. They blamed the president. People wished they had never gotten into "Mr. Madison's War." But the president was still **reelected** that fall.

Here We Go Again

In 1813, the Americans decided to attack Canada again. Their attempts went nowhere. The generals in charge were hopeless. Battle plans were badly prepared. The troops were short of supplies.

In September, things finally changed. American Commodore Oliver Hazard Perry was sent to break through a blockade on Lake Erie. His crew quickly built a few ships. Then Perry led the small fleet into the Battle of Lake Erie. Perry's ship was damaged. He hopped into a rowboat and moved to another ship. The Americans were inspired by his bravery and won the day.

▼ The *Chesapeake* and the *Shannon* at sea

Inspirational Words

There were few great naval battles in 1813. American warships were stuck in port because of the blockade. But there was one big battle in June. The British ship *Shannon* captured the American *Chesapeake* outside Boston Harbor. The American captain, James Lawrence, was wounded during the battle. His last words were, "Don't give up the ship!" This became a rallying cry for Americans.

A Great Leader Falls

The British were not alone at Fort Detroit. About 1,000 Indians had joined them there. One of them was the great Tecumseh. He was one of many Indians who died at the Battle of the Thames. With his death, the Indians lost their spirit. They gave in to the settlers who kept moving west.

▲ The Battle of the Thames, where Tecumseh died

Later, Commodore Perry reported the victory. His famous words were, "We have met the enemy, and they are ours."

The Americans also wanted to take back Fort Detroit. William Henry Harrison marched a large army there. The British panicked. They left and ran toward Canada. The Americans chased them. The two armies met in the Battle of the Thames (TEMZ). The Americans won easily. They captured hundreds of British soldiers.

The war entered its second winter. Things in Canada were about the same as when the war started.

No More Distractions

Great Britain and France stopped fighting each other in 1814. Then, the British put all their attention on America. They decided to go on the attack. The British wanted to bring a quick end to the war.

In August, British ships sailed up the Patuxent (puh-TUCKS-uhnt) and Potomac (puh-TOE-muck) Rivers. Their target was Washington, D.C. The large army came ashore. It marched toward the capital city. The American defense was not organized. It could not stop the British. President Madison and his aides fled the city.

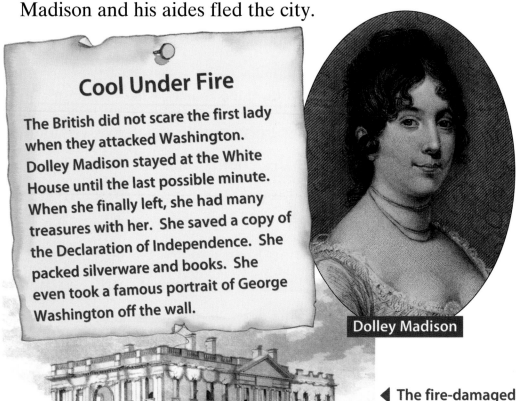

Cool Under Fire

The British did not scare the first lady when they attacked Washington. Dolley Madison stayed at the White House until the last possible minute. When she finally left, she had many treasures with her. She saved a copy of the Declaration of Independence. She packed silverware and books. She even took a famous portrait of George Washington off the wall.

Dolley Madison

◀ The fire-damaged White House

The British entered the capital on August 24. The city was deserted. At the White House, British soldiers found dinner still sitting on the dining room table. They ate it. Then, they set fire to the house.

Other public buildings were also **torched**. Troops used axes to chop up the desks in the House of Representatives and the Senate. Then they set fire to the capitol building. Only a lucky rainstorm kept the building from burning to the ground.

The British left Washington in flames. They headed toward a new target, Baltimore, Maryland. Unlike the capital, this city was ready.

Fresh Coat of Paint

Did you ever wonder where the White House got its name? At first, people called it the President's Palace or the President's House. The house was unique because it was made of white stones. Most buildings in Washington were made of brick. So a few people started calling the mansion (MAN-shuhn) the "White House." After 1814, the house needed a lot of repairs. The burned walls were painted white. Then even more people started calling it the White House. President Theodore Roosevelt made this the official name of the house in 1901.

▲ The capital city under attack by the British

▲ Ships were important during many battles of the War of 1812. This painting shows a key battle on Lake Champlain near Plattsburgh, New York.

America Gets Tough

The Americans sunk dozens of boats at the entrance to Baltimore Harbor. The boats blocked the harbor. Britain's big ships could not sail past the sunken boats to attack Fort McHenry.

The British decided to fire on the fort from far away. They hoped to knock out the fort's cannons. Then, small British ships could slowly make their way into the harbor.

The attack began on September 13, 1814. The British pounded the fort with 2,000 cannonballs. But, the Americans did not surrender. The British had to draw back.

The battle was a huge victory for the United States. It also inspired a famous song. Francis Scott Key was a lawyer from Washington. He had come to Baltimore to ask the British to release a doctor they held prisoner. The British agreed. But, they made the men stay on their ship overnight. The attack on Baltimore was about to begin. The British did not want anyone to warn the soldiers at Fort McHenry.

Key watched the attack throughout the night. He could not tell what was happening. In the morning, he looked across the harbor through rain and smoke. He could just make out the American flag still flying high. Thrilled, he sat down to write a poem called "The Star Spangled Banner."

"Oh, Say, Can You See..."

Soon, Key's poem, "The Star Spangled Banner," was set to music. It became a popular song. Other patriotic songs were just as popular. Two favorites were *Yankee Doodle* and *Hail Columbia. The Star Spangled Banner* did not become the national anthem until 1916. At that time, President Woodrow Wilson made it the official song of the nation.

◄ Francis Scott Key wrote this poem the day after he watched the British attack Baltimore.

The Final Days of War

Both Great Britain and America were tired of war. They sent men to a city called Ghent, in Belgium, for peace talks. At first the meeting did not go well. The British had many demands.

Then, the British heard about the latest American victories. Their enemy was getting stronger and smarter. The British decided to end the war.

Both sides signed the Treaty of Ghent on December 24, 1814. The war was over. But nobody across the ocean in America knew this. The news had to travel by ship. That took weeks.

▼ **Signing the Treaty of Ghent**

▲ Andrew Jackson led the Americans at the Battle of New Orleans.

The British had already begun an attack on Louisiana. They brought in thousands of soldiers. These men were experienced from the war against France. On January 8, 1815, the troops attacked New Orleans.

The American forces looked like they were in trouble. Their leader, Andrew Jackson, had a much smaller army. It was a "rag-tag" group of **militia** (muh-LISH-uh), Choctaw (CHOLK-taw) Indians, freed slaves, and pirates. Somehow, this group surprised everyone. The British had more than 2,000 men killed or wounded. The Americans lost only a few.

Good Times for the U.S.A.

The Americans finally learned about the Treaty of Ghent in February 1815. They were happy the war was over.

The treaty left things just like they were when the war started. All territories were returned to their original countries. Neither side won or lost anything.

Nothing was said about the fact that the British had been stopping American ships. Also, the treaty did not mention the impressment of seamen. But Great Britain never tried these things again.

Sad Days to Come

In some ways, the War of 1812 helped lead to the Civil War. It opened up new territories for white settlers in the South and West. These became new slave states. The country became more evenly divided between slave and free states. Neither side could overpower the other.

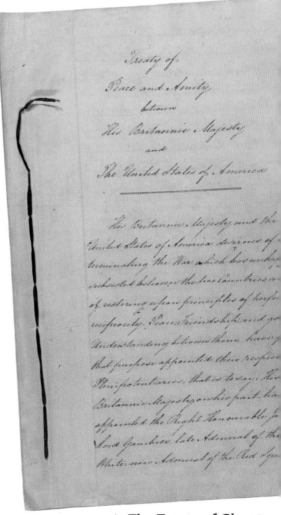

▲ The Treaty of Ghent

The next few years were a great time for the United States. The people were proud of their performance in the war. There were no more shipping problems to worry about. Trade boomed. People built homes and businesses. Some called this time "The **Era** of Good Feelings."

People around the world admired America for standing up to Great Britain. They looked at the young country in a new way. America did not really win the War of 1812. But, it did win the respect of Great Britain and the world. In that way, it really was a second war for American independence.

The Real Losers

The Indians were the ones who really lost this war. Their great leader, Tecumseh, was killed. The Indians also lost a lot of land. They no longer had the help of the British in Canada. The Indians were not able to fight the movement of white settlers onto their lands.

◀ This image symbolizes the peace between the two nations after the War of 1812.

Glossary

ambassadors—people who officially represent their government to other countries

blockade—using ships to keep a country from sailing any of its ships into or out of port

compromiser—a person who solves an argument by giving each side part of what it wants

democracy—a government run by the people

deserted—ran away from the military when you were supposed to still serve

embargo—a government order that outlaws trading with other countries

era—a period of time

fleet—a group of warships that are under the same commander

frigate—a medium-sized warship

honorable—deserving of respect

impressed—forced to join the military

independence—standing on your own without help from anyone

mansion—a large house

militia—an army made up of ordinary people who are not paid to be soldiers

national anthem—a song that states the patriotic feelings of a country

nationalism—thinking that the needs and customs of your country are more important than those of any other country

patriotic—feeling love for one's country

politicians—people who run for office

rallying cry—words that are used to excite and encourage people to do something

reelected—won another term in office

seize—to take quickly

slogan—words that express what a group believes or wants

surrender—to give up

territory—areas of land controlled by a country, but outside the borders of the country

torched—set on fire

treaty—an agreement between countries